ॐ

THE GEETA

THE GEETĀ

The Gospel
of the Lord Shri Krishna

put into English

from the original Sanskrit by

Shri Purohit Swāmi

with a preface by

His Highness

Sir Sayāji Rāo Gaekwār

The Mahārājā of Barodā
G.C.S.I., G.C.I.E.
Senā-Khās-Khel, Samsher-Bahādur
Doulat-E-Englishia

Faber and Faber Limited
London and Boston

First published in 1935
by Faber and Faber Limited
3 Queen Square London W.C.1
First published in this edition 1965
Reprinted 1969, 1973 and 1978
Printed in Great Britain
at the Alden Press, Oxford
All rights reserved

ISBN 0 571 06157 5

To my friend William Butler Yeats,

They say that East and West 'shall never meet', but forget history. The West has captured the East materially, the East has captured the West spiritually, and it is only in Spirit that there has been, or can be, meeting. You had vision; you saw truth; you proclaimed it. The East is grateful, the West should be.

Accept this Geetā, the Upanishads in essence, a humble offering on your seventieth birthday. Revealed, according to our Indian tradition, five thousand and thirty-six years ago, it has consoled millions, inspired philosophers and prophets.

I admire your conviction, your courage; I adore your friendship, your devotion; I love your sincerity, your sacrifice.

May the Lord bless you, that Lord in whom India has found her rest.

PUROHIT SWĀMI
Ever in service.

London
13 *June* 1935

PREFACE

★

I recommend this beautiful translation of one of the greatest philosophical poems of the world to the English-speaking public. The Geetā is to Hindus what the Bible is to Christians, the Koran to Muslims. It is perhaps, however, unique among sacred books in that it deals not only with man's spiritual and moral difficulties but with those that are intellectual. Generations have found its intellectual unification of experience the framework wherein they can fit the observations and discoveries of their lives. It satisfies the whole man.

SAYĀJI RĀO GAEKWĀR

CONTENTS

★

THE GEETĀ

CHAPTER I

★

The King Dhritarāshtra asked: O Sanjaya! What happened on the sacred battlefield of Kurukshetra, when my people gathered against the Pāndavās?

Sanjaya replied: The Prince Duryôdhana, when he saw the army of the Pāndavās paraded, approached his preceptor Guru Drôna and spoke as follows:

'Revered Father! Behold this mighty host of the Pāndavās, paraded by the son of King Drupada, thy wise disciple.

'In it are heroes and great bowmen; the equals in battle of Arjuna and Bheema, Yuyudhāna, Virāta and Drupada, great soldiers all;

'Dhrishtaketu, Chekitān, the valiant King of Benāres, Purujit, Kuntibhôja, Shaibya—a master over many;

'Yudhāmanyu, Uttamoujā, Soubhadra, and the sons of Droupadi, famous men.

'Further, take note of all those captains who have ranged themselves on our side, O best of Spiritual Guides! the leaders of my army. I will name them for you.

'You come first; then Bheeshma, Karna, Kripa, great soldiers; Ashwaththāmā, Vikarna, and the son of Sômadatta;

'And many others, all ready to die for my sake, all armed, all skilled in war.

15

'Yet our army seems the weaker, though commanded by Bheeshma, their army seems the stronger, though commanded by Bheema.

'Therefore in the rank and file, let all stand firm in their posts, according to battalions; and all you generals about Bheeshma.'

Then to enliven his spirits, the brave Grandfather Bheeshma, eldest of the Kuru-clan, blew his conch, till it sounded like a lion's roar.

And immediately all the conches and drums, the trumpets and horns, blared forth in tumultuous uproar.

Then seated in their spacious war-chariot, yoked with white horses, Lord Shri Krishna and Arjuna sounded their divine shells.

Lord Shri Krishna blew His Pānchajanya and Arjuna his Devadatta, brave Bheema his renowned shell, Poundra.

The King Dharmarāja, the son of Kunti, blew the Anantavijaya, Nakula and Sahadeo, the Sughôsh and Manipushpaka respectively.

And the Mahārājā of Benāres the great archer, Shikhandi the great soldier, Dhrishtadyumna, Virāta and Sātyaki the invincible,

And O King! Drupada, the sons of Droupadi, and Soubhadra the great soldier, blew their conches.

The tumult rent the hearts of the sons of Dhritarāshtra, and violently shook heaven and earth with its echo.

Then beholding the sons of Dhritarāshtra, drawn up on the battlefield, ready to begin the fight, Arjuna, whose flag bore the Hanumān,

Raising his bow, spoke thus to the Lord Shri Krishna: 'O Infallible! Lord of the earth! please draw up my chariot betwixt the two armies,

'So that I may observe those who must fight on my side, those who must fight against me;

'And gaze over this array of soldiers, eager to please the sinful son of Dhritarāshtra.'

Sanjaya said: Having listened to the request of Arjuna, Lord Shri Krishna drew up His bright chariot exactly in the midst between the two armies,

Whither Bheeshma and Drôna had led all the rulers of the earth, and spoke thus: 'O Arjuna! Behold these members of the family of Kuru assembled.'

There Arjuna noticed fathers, grandfathers, uncles, cousins, sons, grandsons, teachers, friends;

Fathers-in-law and benefactors, arrayed on both sides. Arjuna then gazed at all those kinsmen before him.

And his heart melted with pity and sadly he spoke: 'O my Lord! When I see all these, my own people, thirsting for battle,

'My limbs fail me and my throat is parched, my body trembles and my hair stands on end.

'The bow Gāndeeva slips from my hand, and my skin burns. I cannot keep quiet, for my mind is in a tumult.

'The omens are adverse; what good can come from the slaughter of my people on this battlefield?

'Ah, my Lord! I crave not for victory, nor for kingdom, nor for any pleasure. What were a kingdom or happiness or life to me,

'When those for whose sake I desire these things stand here about to sacrifice their property and their lives:

'Teachers, fathers, and grandfathers, sons and grandsons, uncles, fathers-in-law, brothers-in-law, and other relatives.

'I would not kill them, even for the three worlds; why then for this poor earth? It matters not, if I myself am killed.

'My Lord! What happiness can come from the death of these sons of Dhritarāshtra? We shall sin if we kill these desperate men.

'We are worthy of a nobler feat than to slaughter our relatives—the sons of Dhritarāshtra; for, my Lord! how can we be happy if we kill our kinsmen?

'Although these men, blinded by greed, see no guilt in destroying their kin, or fighting against their friends,

'Should not we, whose eyes are open, who consider it to be wrong to annihilate our house, turn away from so great a crime?

'The destruction of our kindred means the destruction of the traditions of our ancient lineage, and when these are lost, irreligion will overrun our homes.

'When irreligion spreads, the women of the house begin to stray; when they lose their purity, adulteration of the stock follows.

'Promiscuity ruins both the family and those who defile it; while the souls of our ancestors droop, through lack of the funeral cakes and ablutions.

'By the destruction of our lineage and the pollution of blood, ancient class traditions and family purity alike perish.

'The wise say, my Lord! that they are forever lost, whose ancient traditions are lost.

'Alas, it is strange that we should be willing to kill our own countrymen and commit a great sin, in order to enjoy the pleasures of a kingdom.

'If, on the contrary, the sons of Dhritarāshtra, with weapons in their hands, should slay me, unarmed and unresisting, surely that would be better for my welfare!'

Sanjaya said: Having spoken thus, in the midst of the armies, Arjuna sank on the seat of the chariot, casting away his bow and arrow, heart-broken with grief.

Thus, in the Holy Book the Bhagavad-Geetā, one of the Upanishads, in the Science of the Supreme Spirit, in the Art of Self-Knowledge, in the colloquy between the Divine Lord Shri Krishna and the Prince Arjuna, stands the first chapter, entitled: The Despondency of Arjuna.

CHAPTER II

★

Sanjaya then told how the Lord Shri Krishna, seeing Arjuna overwhelmed with compassion, his eyes dimmed with flowing tears and full of despondency, consoled him:

The Lord said: 'My beloved friend! Why yield, just on the eve of battle, to this weakness which does no credit to those who call themselves Aryans, and only brings them infamy and bars against them the gates of heaven?

'O Arjuna! Why give way to unmanliness? O thou who art the terror of thine enemies! Shake off such shameful effeminacy, make ready to act!'

Arjuna argued: 'My Lord! How can I, when the battle rages, send an arrow through Bheeshma and Dróna, who should receive my reverence?

'Rather would I content myself with a beggar's crust than kill these teachers of mine, these precious noble souls! To slay these masters who are my benefactors would be to stain the sweetness of life's pleasure with their blood.

'Nor can I say whether it were better that they conquer me or for me to conquer them, since I would no longer care to live if I killed these sons of Dhritarāshtra, now preparing for fight.

'My heart is oppressed with pity; and my mind confused as to what my duty is. Therefore, my Lord! tell me what is best for my spiritual welfare; for I am Thy disciple. Please direct me, I pray.

'For should I attain the monarchy of the visible world, or

20

over the invisible world, it would not drive away the anguish which is now paralysing my senses.'

Sanjaya continued: Arjuna, the conqueror of all enemies, then told the Lord of All-Hearts that he would not fight, and became silent, O King!

Thereupon the Lord, with a gracious smile, addressed him who was so much depressed in the midst between the two armies.

Lord Shri Krishna said: 'Why grieve for those for whom no grief is due, and yet profess wisdom. The wise grieve neither for the dead nor for the living.

'There was never a time when I was not, nor thou, nor these princes were not; there will never be a time when we shall cease to be.

'As the soul experiences in this body, infancy, youth and old age, so finally it passes into another. The wise have no delusion about this.

'Those external relations which bring cold and heat, pain and happiness, they come and go; they are not permanent. Endure them bravely, O Prince!

'The hero whose soul is unmoved by circumstance, who accepts pleasure and pain with equanimity, only he is fit for immortality.

'That which is not, shall never be; that which is, shall never cease to be. To the wise, these truths are self-evident.

'The Spirit, which pervades all that we see, is imperishable. Nothing can destroy the Spirit.

'The material bodies which this Eternal, Indestructible, Immeasurable Spirit inhabits are all finite. Therefore fight, O Valiant Man!

'He who thinks that the Spirit kills, and he who thinks of It as killed, are both ignorant. The Spirit kills not, nor is It killed.

'It was not born; It will never die: nor once having been, can It ever cease to be: Unborn, Eternal, Ever-enduring, yet Most Ancient, the Spirit dies not when the body is dead.

'He who knows the Spirit as Indestructible, Immortal, Unborn, Always-the-Same, how should he kill or cause to be killed?

'As a man discards his threadbare robes and puts on new, so the Spirit throws off Its worn-out bodies and takes fresh ones.

'Weapons cleave It not, fire burns It not, water drenches It not and wind dries It not.

'It is impenetrable; It can be neither drowned nor scorched nor dried. It is Eternal, All-pervading, Unchanging, Immovable and Most Ancient.

'It is named the Unmanifest, the Unthinkable, the Immutable. Wherefore, knowing the Spirit as such, thou hast no cause to grieve.

'Even if thou thinkest of It as constantly being born, constantly dying; even then, O Mighty Man! thou still hast no cause to grieve.

'For death is as sure for that which is born, as birth is for that which is dead. Therefore grieve not for what is inevitable.

'The end and beginning of beings are unknown. We see only the intervening formations. Then what cause is there for grief?

'One hears of the Spirit with surprise, another thinks It marvellous, the third listens without comprehending. Thus, though many are told about It, scarcely is there one who knows It.

'Be not anxious about these armies. The Spirit in man is imperishable.

'Thou must look at thy duty. Nothing can be more welcome to a soldier than a righteous war. Therefore to waver in thy resolve is unworthy, O Arjuna!

'Blessed are the soldiers who find their opportunity. This opportunity has opened for thee the gates of heaven.

'Refuse to fight in this righteous cause, and thou wilt be a traitor, lost to fame, incurring only sin.

'Men will talk forever of thy disgrace; and to the noble, dishonour is worse than death.

'Great generals will think that thou hast fled from the battlefield through cowardice, though once honoured thou wilt seem despicable.

'Thine enemies will spread scandal, and mock at thy courage. Can anything be more humiliating?

'If killed, thou shalt attain Heaven; if victorious, enjoy the kingdom of earth. Therefore arise, O son of Kunti! and fight.

'Look upon pleasure and pain, victory and defeat, with an equal eye. Make ready for the combat, and thou shalt commit no sin.

'I have told thee the philosophy of Knowledge. Now listen! and I will explain the philosophy of Action, by means of which, O Arjuna, thou shalt break through the bondage of all action.

'On this Path, endeavour is never wasted, nor can it ever be repressed. Even a very little of its practice protects one from great danger.

'By its means, the straying intellect becomes steadied in the contemplation of one object only; whereas the minds of the irresolute stray into bypaths innumerable.

'Only the ignorant speak in figurative language. It is they

who extol the letter of the scriptures, saying —"There is nothing deeper than this."

'Consulting only their desires, they construct their own heaven, devising arduous and complex rites to secure their own pleasure and their own power; and the only result is rebirth.

'While their minds are absorbed with ideas of power and personal enjoyment, they cannot concentrate their discrimination on one point.

'The Vedic Scriptures tell of the three constituents of life— the Qualities. Rise above all of them, O Arjuna! above all the pairs of opposing sensations; be steady in truth, free from worldly anxieties, and centred in the Self.

'As a man can drink water from any side of a full tank, so the skilled theologian can wrest from any scripture that which will serve his purpose.

'But thou hast only the right to work; but none to the fruit thereof. Let not then the fruit of thy action be thy motive; nor yet be thou enamoured of inaction.

'Perform all thy actions with mind concentrated on the Divine, renouncing attachment and looking upon success and failure with an equal eye. Spirituality implies equanimity.

'Physical action is far inferior to an intellect concentrated on the Divine. Have recourse then to the Pure Intelligence. It is only the petty-minded who work for reward.

'When a man attains to Pure Reason, he renounces in this world the results of good and evil alike. Cling thou to Right Action. Spirituality is the real art of living.

'The sages guided by Pure Intellect renounce the fruit of action; and, freed from the chains of rebirth, they reach the highest bliss.

'When thy reason has crossed the entanglements of illusion,

then shalt thou become indifferent both to the philosophies thou hast heard, and to those thou mayest yet hear.

'When the intellect, bewildered by the multiplicity of holy scripts, stands unperturbed in blissful contemplation of the Infinite, then hast thou attained Spirituality.'

Arjuna asked: 'My Lord! How can we recognise the saint who has attained Pure Intellect, who has reached this state of Bliss, and whose mind is steady? How does he talk, how does he live and how does he act?'

Lord Shri Krishna replied: 'When a man has given up the desires of his heart and is satisfied with the Self alone, be sure that he has reached the highest state.

'The sage, whose mind is unruffled in suffering, whose desire is not roused by enjoyment, who is without attachment, anger or fear—take him to be one who stands at that lofty level.

'He who wherever he goes is attached to no person and to no place by ties of flesh; who accepts good and evil alike, neither welcoming the one nor shrinking from the other—take him to be one who is merged in the Infinite.

'He who can withdraw his senses from the attraction of their objects, as the tortoise draws his limbs within his shell —take it that such an one has attained Perfection.

'The objects of sense turn from him who is abstemious. Even the relish for them is lost in him who has seen the Truth.

'O Arjuna! The mind of him, who is trying to conquer it, is forcibly carried away in spite of his efforts, by his tumultuous senses.

'Restraining them all, let him meditate steadfastly on Me; for who thus conquers his senses achieves perfection.

'When a man dwells on the objects of sense, he creates an

attraction for them; attraction develops into desire, and desire breeds anger.

'Anger induces delusion; delusion, loss of memory; through loss of memory, reason is shattered; and loss of reason leads to destruction.

'But the self-controlled soul, who moves amongst sense-objects, free from either attachment or repulsion, he wins eternal Peace.

'Having attained Peace, he becomes free from misery; for when the mind gains peace, right discrimination follows.

'Right discrimination is not for him who cannot concentrate. Without concentration, there cannot be meditation; he who cannot meditate must not expect peace; and without peace, how can anyone expect happiness?

'As a ship at sea is tossed by the tempest, so the reason is carried away by the mind when preyed upon by the straying senses.

'Therefore, O Mighty-in-Arms! he who keeps his senses detached from their objects—take it that his reason is purified.

'The saint is awake when the world sleeps, and he ignores that for which the world lives.

'He attains Peace, into whom desires flow as rivers into the ocean, which though brimming with water remains ever the same; not he whom desire carries away.

'He attains Peace who, giving up desire, moves through the world without aspiration, possessing nothing which he can call his own, and free from pride.

'O Arjuna! This is the state of the Self, the Supreme Spirit, to which if a man once attain, it shall never be taken from him. Even at the time of leaving the body, he will remain firmly enthroned there, and will become one with the Eternal.'

Thus, in the Holy Book the Bhagavad-Geetā, one of the Upanishads, in the Science of the Supreme Spirit, in the Art of Self-Knowledge, in the colloquy between the Divine Lord Shri Krishna and the Prince Arjuna, stands the second chapter, entitled: The Philosophy of Discrimination.

CHAPTER III

★

Arjuna questioned: 'My Lord! If wisdom is above action, why dost Thou advise me to engage in this terrible fight?

'Thy language perplexes me and confuses my reason. Therefore please tell me the only way by which I may, without doubt, secure my spiritual welfare.'

Lord Shri Krishna replied: 'In this world, as I have said, there is a twofold path, O Sinless One! There is the Path of Wisdom for those who meditate, and the Path of Action for those who work.

'No man can attain freedom from activity by refraining from action; nor can he reach perfection by merely refusing to act.

'He cannot even for a moment remain really inactive; for the Qualities of Nature will compel him to act whether he will or no.

'He who remains motionless, refusing to act, but all the while brooding over sensuous objects, that deluded soul is simply a hypocrite.

'But, O Arjuna! All honour to him whose mind controls his senses; for he is thereby beginning to practise Karma-Yôga, the Path of Right Action, keeping himself always unattached.

'Do thy duty as prescribed; for action for duty's sake is superior to inaction. Even the maintenance of the body would be impossible if man remained inactive.

'In this world people are fettered by action, unless it is performed as a sacrifice. Therefore, O Arjuna! let thy acts be done without attachment, as sacrifice only.

'In the beginning, when God created all beings by the sacrifice of Himself, He said unto them: "Through sacrifice you can procreate, and it shall satisfy all your desires.

' "Worship the Powers of Nature thereby, and let them nourish you in return; thus supporting each other, you shall attain your highest welfare.

' "For, fed on sacrifice, Nature will give you all the enjoyment you can desire. But he who enjoys what she gives without returning is, indeed, a robber."

'The sages who enjoy the food that remains after the sacrifice is made, are freed from all sin; but the selfish who spread their feast only for themselves feed on sin only.

'All creatures are the product of food, food is the product of rain, rain comes by sacrifice, and sacrifice is the noblest form of action.

'All action originates in the Supreme Spirit, which is Imperishable, and in sacrificial action the all-pervading Spirit is consciously present.

'Thus he who does not help the revolving wheel of sacrifice, but instead leads a sinful life, rejoicing in the gratification of his senses, O Arjuna! he breathes in vain.

'On the other hand, the soul who meditates on the Self, is content to serve the Self, and rests satisfied within the Self; there remains nothing more for him to accomplish.

'He has nothing to gain by the performance or non-performance of action. His welfare depends not on any contribution that an earthly creature can make.

'Therefore do thy duty perfectly, without care for the results; for he who does his duty disinterestedly attains the Supreme.

'King Janaka and others attained perfection through action alone. Even for the sake of enlightening the world, it is thy duty to act;

'For whatever a great man does, others imitate. People conform to the standard which he has set.

'There is nothing in this universe, O Arjuna! that I am compelled to do; nor anything for Me to attain; yet I am persistently active.

'For were I not to act without ceasing, O Prince! people would be glad to do likewise.

'And if I were to refrain from action, the human race would be ruined; I should lead the world to chaos, and destruction would follow.

'As the ignorant act, because of their fondness for action, so should the wise act without such attachment, fixing their eyes, O Arjuna! only on the welfare of the world.

'But a wise man should not perturb the minds of the ignorant, who are attached to action; let him perform his own actions in the right spirit, with concentration on Me, thus inspiring all to do the same.

'Action is the product of the Qualities inherent in Nature. It is only the ignorant man who, misled by personal egotism, says: "I am the doer."

'But he, O Mighty One! who understands correctly the relation of the Qualities to action, is not attached to the act, for he perceives that it is merely the action and reaction of the Qualities among themselves.

'Those who do not understand the Qualities are interested in the act. Still, the wise man who knows the truth should not disturb the mind of him who does not.

'Therefore, surrendering thy actions unto Me, thy thoughts concentrated on the Absolute, free from selfishness and without anticipation of reward, with mind devoid of excitement, begin thou to fight.

'Those who act always in accordance with My precepts, firm in faith and without cavilling, they too are freed from the bondage of action.

'But they who ridicule My word and do not keep it, are ignorant, devoid of wisdom, and blind. They seek but their own destruction.

'Even the wise man acts in character with his nature; indeed, all creatures act according to their natures. What is the use of compulsion then?

'The love and hate which are aroused by the objects of sense arise from Nature; do not yield to them. They only obstruct the path.

'It is better to do thine own duty, however lacking in merit, than to do that of another, even though efficiently. It is better to die doing one's own duty, for to do the duty of another is fraught with danger.'

Arjuna asked: 'My Lord! Tell me, what is it that drives a man to sin, even against his will and as if by compulsion?'

Lord Shri Krishna said: 'It is desire, it is aversion, born of passion. Desire consumes and corrupts everything. It is man's greatest enemy.

'As fire is shrouded in smoke, a mirror by dust, and a child by the womb, so is the universe enveloped in desire.

'It is the wise man's constant enemy; it tarnishes the face of wisdom. It is as insatiable as a flame of fire.

'It works through the senses, the mind and the reason; and with their help destroys wisdom and confounds the soul.

'Therefore, O Arjuna! first control thy senses, and then slay desire; for it is full of sin, and is the destroyer of knowledge and of wisdom.

'It is said that the senses are powerful. But beyond the senses is the mind, beyond mind is intellect, and beyond and greater than intellect is He.

'Thus, O Mighty-in-Arms! knowing Him to be beyond the intellect and, by His help, subduing thy personal egotism, kill thine enemy, Desire, extremely difficult though it be.'

Thus, in the Holy Book the Bhagavad-Geetā, one of the Upanishads, in the Science of the Supreme Spirit, in the Art of Self-Knowledge, in the colloquy between the Divine Lord Shri Krishna and the Prince Arjuna, stands the third chapter entitled: Karma-Yôga or The Path of Action.

CHAPTER IV

★

Lord Shri Krishna said: 'This imperishable philosophy I taught to Viwaswāna the founder of the Sun-dynasty, Viwaswāna gave it to Manu the Lawgiver, and Manu to King Ikshwāku!

'The Divine Kings knew it, for it was their tradition. Then, after a long time, at last it was forgotten.

'It is this same ancient Path that I have now revealed to thee, since thou art My devotee and My friend. It is the supreme Secret.'

Arjuna asked: 'My Lord! Viwaswāna was born before Thee; how then canst Thou have revealed it to him?'

Lord Shri Krishna replied: 'I have been born again and again, from time to time; thou too, O Arjuna! My births are known to Me, but thou knowest not thine.

'I have no beginning. Though I am imperishable, as well as Lord of all that exists, yet by My own will and power do I manifest Myself.

'Whenever spirituality decays and materialism is rampant, then, O Arjuna! I reincarnate Myself.

'To protect the righteous, to destroy the wicked, and to establish the kingdom of God, I am reborn from age to age.

'He who realises the divine truth concerning My birth and life, is not born again; and when he leaves his body, he becomes one with Me.

'Many have merged their existence in Mine, being freed

33

from desire, fear and anger, filled always with Me, and purified by the illuminating flame of self-abnegation.

'Howsoever men try to worship Me, so do I welcome them. By whatever path they travel, it leads to Me at last.

'Those who look for success, worship the Powers; and in this world their actions bear immediate fruit.

'The four divisions of society (the wise, the soldier, the merchant, the labourer) were created by Me, according to the natural distribution of Qualities and instincts. I am the author of them, though I Myself do no action, and am changeless.

'My actions do not fetter Me, nor do I desire anything that they can bring. He who thus realises Me is not enslaved by action.

'In the light of this wisdom, our ancestors, who sought deliverance, performed their acts. Act thou also, as did our fathers of old.

'What is action and what is inaction? It is a question which has bewildered the wise. But I will declare unto thee the philosophy of action, and knowing it, thou shalt be free from evil.

'It is necessary to consider what is right action, what is wrong action, and what is inaction; for mysterious is the law of action.

He who can see inaction in action, and action in inaction, is the wisest among men. He is a saint, even though he still acts.

'The wise call him a sage; for whatever he undertakes is free from the motive of desire, and his deeds are purified by the fire of Wisdom.

'Having surrendered all claim to the results of his actions, always contented and independent, in reality he does nothing, even though he is apparently acting.

'Expecting nothing, his mind and personality controlled, without greed, doing bodily actions only; though he acts, yet he remains untainted.

'Content with what comes to him without effort of his own, mounting above the pairs of opposites, free from envy, his mind balanced both in success and failure, though he act, yet the consequences do not bind him.

'He who is without attachment, free, his mind centred in wisdom, his actions, being done as a sacrifice, leave no trace behind.

'For him, the sacrifice itself is the Spirit; the Spirit and the oblation are one; it is the Spirit Itself which is sacrificed in Its own fire, and the man even in action is united with God, since while performing his act, his mind never ceases to be fixed on Him.

'Some sages sacrifice to the Powers; others offer themselves on the altar of the Eternal.

'Some sacrifice their physical senses in the fire of self-control; others offer up their contact with external objects in the sacrificial fire of their senses.

'Others again sacrifice their activities and their vitality in the Spiritual fire of self-abnegation, kindled by wisdom.

'And yet others offer as their sacrifice wealth, austerities and meditation. Monks wedded to their vows renounce their scriptural learning, and even their spiritual powers.

'There are some who practise control of the Vital Energy and govern the subtle forces of Prāna and Apāna, thereby sacrificing their Prāna unto Apāna, or their Apāna unto Prāna.

'Others, controlling their diet, sacrifice their worldly life to the spiritual fire. All understand the principle of sacrifice, and by its means their sins are washed away.

'Tasting the nectar of immortality, as the reward of sacrifice, they reach the Eternal. This world is not for those who refuse to sacrifice; much less the other world.

'In this way other sacrifices too may be undergone for the Spirit's sake. Know thou that they all depend on action. Knowing this, thou shalt be free.

'The sacrifice of wisdom is superior to any material sacrifice; for, O Arjuna! the climax of action is always Realisation.

'This shalt thou learn by prostrating thyself at the Master's feet, by questioning Him and by serving Him. The wise who have realised the Truth will teach thee wisdom.

'Having known That, thou shalt never again be confounded; and, O Arjuna! by the power of that wisdom, thou shalt see all these people as it were thine own Self, and therefore as Me.

'Be thou the greatest of all sinners, yet thou shalt cross over all sin by the ferry-boat of wisdom.

'As the kindled fire consumes the fuel, so, O Arjuna! in the flame of wisdom the embers of action are burnt to ashes.

'There is nothing in the world so purifying as wisdom; and he who is a perfect saint finds that at last in his own Self.

'He who is full of faith attains wisdom, and he too who can control his senses. Having attained that wisdom, he shall ere long attain the Supreme Peace.

'But the ignorant man, and he who has no faith, and the sceptic are lost. Neither in this world, nor elsewhere, is there any happiness in store for him who always doubts.

'But the man who has renounced his action for meditation, who has cleft his doubt in twain by the sword of wisdom, who remains always enthroned in his Self, is not bound by his acts.

'Therefore, cleaving asunder with the sword of wisdom the doubts of thy heart, which thine own ignorance has engendered, follow the Path of Wisdom and arise!'

Thus, in the Holy Book the Bhagavad-Geetā, one of the Upanishads, in the Science of the Supreme Spirit, in the Art of Self-Knowledge, in the colloquy between the Divine Lord Shri Krishna and the Prince Arjuna, stands the fourth chapter, entitled: The Dnyāna-Yôga or The Path of Wisdom.

CHAPTER V

★

Arjuna said: 'My Lord! At one moment Thou praisest renunciation of action; at another, right action. Tell me truly, I pray, which of these is the more conducive to my highest welfare?'

Lord Shri Krishna replied: 'Renunciation of action and the path of right action both lead to the highest; of the two, right action is the better.

'He is a true ascetic who never desires or dislikes, who is uninfluenced by the opposites, and is easily freed from bondage.

'Only the unenlightened speak of wisdom and right action as separate; not the wise. If any man knows one, he enjoys the fruit of both.

'The level which is reached by wisdom is attained through right action as well. He who perceives that the two are one, knows the truth.

'Without concentration, O Mighty Man! renunciation is difficult. But the sage who is always meditating on the Divine, before long shall attain the Absolute.

'He who is spiritual, who is pure, who has overcome his senses and his personal self, who has realised his highest Self as the Self of all, such an one, even though he acts, is not bound by his acts.

'Though the saint sees, hears, touches, smells, eats, moves, sleeps and breathes, yet he knows the Truth, and he knows that it is not he who acts.

'Though he talks, though he gives and receives, though he opens his eyes and shuts them, he still knows that his senses are merely disporting themselves among the objects of perception.

'He who dedicates his actions to the Spirit, without any personal attachment to them, he is no more tainted by sin than the water-lily is wetted by water.

'The sage performs his action dispassionately, using his body, mind and intellect, and even his senses, always as a means of purification.

'Having abandoned the fruit of action, he wins eternal peace. Others unacquainted with spirituality, led by desire and clinging to the benefit which they think will follow their actions, become entangled by them.

'Mentally renouncing all actions, the self-controlled soul enjoys bliss in this body, the city of the nine gates, neither doing anything himself, nor causing anything to be done.

'The Lord of this universe has not ordained activity, or any incentive thereto, or any relation between an act and its consequences. All this is the work of Nature.

'The Lord does not accept responsibility for any man's sin or merit. Men are deluded because in them wisdom is submerged in ignorance.

'Surely wisdom is like the sun, revealing the supreme truth to those whose ignorance is dispelled by the wisdom of the Self.

'Meditating on the Divine, having faith in the Divine, concentrating on the Divine, and losing themselves in the Divine, their sins dissolved in wisdom, they go whence there is no return.

'Sages look equally upon all, whether he be a minister of learning and humility, or an infidel, or whether it be a cow, an elephant, or a dog.

'Even in this world they conquer their earth-life whose minds, fixed on the Supreme, remain always balanced; for the Supreme has neither blemish nor bias.

'He who knows and lives in the Absolute remains unmoved and unperturbed; he is not elated by pleasure, or depressed by pain.

'He finds happiness in his own Self, and enjoys eternal bliss, whose heart does not yearn for the contacts of earth, and whose Self is one with the Everlasting.

'The joys that spring from external associations bring pain; they have their beginnings and their endings. The wise man does not rejoice in them.

'He who, before he leaves his body, learns to surmount the promptings of desire and anger, is a saint, and is happy.

'He who is happy within his Self, and has found Its peace, and in whom the inner light shines, that sage attains Eternal·Bliss and becomes the Spirit Itself.

'Sages whose sins have been washed away, whose sense of separateness has vanished, who have subdued themselves, and seek only the welfare of all, come to the Eternal Spirit.

'Saints who know their Selves, who control their minds, and feel neither desire nor anger, find Eternal Bliss everywhere.

'Excluding external objects, his gaze fixed between the eyebrows, the inward and outward breathings passing equally through his nostrils;

'Governing sense, mind and intellect, intent on liberation, free from desire, fear and anger, the sage is forever free.

'Knowing me as Him who gladly receives all offerings of austerity and sacrifice, as the Mighty Ruler of all the Worlds, and the Friend of all beings, he passes to Eternal Peace.'

Thus, in the Holy Book the Bhagavad-Geetā, one of the Upanishads, in the Science of the Supreme Spirit, in the Art of Self-Knowledge, in the colloquy between the Divine Lord Shri Krishna and the Prince Arjuna, stands the fifth chapter, entitled: The Renunciation of Action.

CHAPTER VI

★

Lord Shri Krishna said: 'He who acts because it is his duty, not thinking of the consequences, is really spiritual and a true ascetic; and not he who merely observes rituals or who shuns all action.

'O Arjuna! Renunciation is in fact what is called Right Action. No one can become spiritual who has not renounced all desire.

'For the sage who seeks the heights of spiritual meditation, practice is the only method, and when he has attained them, he must maintain himself there by continual self-control.

'When a man renounces even the thought of initiating action, when he is not interested in sense-objects or any results which may flow from his acts, then in truth he understands spirituality.

'Let him seek liberation by the help of his highest Self, and let him never disgrace his own Self. For that Self is his only friend; yet it may also be his enemy.

'To him who has conquered his lower nature by Its help, the Self is a friend, but to him who has not done so, It is an enemy.

'The Self of him who is self-controlled and has attained peace, is equally unmoved by heat or cold, pleasure or pain, honour or dishonour.

'He who desires nothing but wisdom and spiritual insight, who has conquered his senses and who looks with the same eye upon a lump of earth, a stone or fine gold, is the real saint.

'He looks impartially on all—lover, friend, or foe; indifferent or hostile; alien or relative; virtuous or sinful.

'Let the student of spirituality try unceasingly to concentrate his mind; let him live in seclusion, absolutely alone, with mind and personality controlled, free from desire, and without possessions.

'Having chosen a holy place, let him sit in a firm posture on a seat, neither too high nor too low, and covered with a grass mat, a deer skin and a cloth.

'Seated thus, his mind concentrated, its functions controlled, and his senses governed, let him practise meditation for the purification of his lower nature.

'Let him hold body, head and neck erect, motionless and steady; let him look fixedly at the tip of his nose, turning neither to the right nor to the left.

'With peace in his heart and no fear, observing the vow of celibacy, with mind controlled and fixed on Me, let the student lose himself in contemplation of Me.

'Thus keeping his mind always in communion with Me, and with his thoughts subdued, he shall attain that Peace which is Mine and which will lead him to liberation at last.

'Meditation is not for him who eats too much, nor for him who eats not at all: nor for him who is overmuch addicted to sleep, nor for him who is always awake.

'But for him who regulates his food and recreation, who is balanced in action, in sleep and in waking, it shall dispel all unhappiness.

'When the mind, completely controlled, is centred in the Self, and free from all earthly desires, then is the man truly spiritual.

'The wise man who has conquered his mind and is absorbed in the Self is as a lamp which does not flicker, since it stands sheltered from every wind.

'There, where the whole nature is seen in the light of the Self, where the man abides within his Self and is satisfied, there, its functions restrained by its union with the Divine, the mind finds rest.

'When he enjoys the Bliss which passes sense, and which only the Pure Intellect can grasp, when he comes to rest within his own highest Self, never again will he stray from reality.

'Finding That, he will realise that there is no possession so precious. And when once established there, no calamity can disturb him.

'This inner severance from the affliction of misery is spirituality. It should be practised with determination, and with a heart which refuses to be depressed.

'Renouncing every desire which imagination can conceive, controlling the senses at every point by the power of mind:

'Little by little, by the help of his reason controlled by fortitude, let him attain peace; and, fixing his mind on the Self, let him not think of any other thing.

'When the volatile and wavering mind would wander, let him restrain it, and bring it again to its allegiance to the Self.

'Supreme Bliss is the lot of the sage, whose mind attains Peace, whose passions subside, who is without sin, and who becomes one with the Absolute.

'Thus, free from sin, abiding always in the Eternal, the saint enjoys without effort the Bliss which flows from realisation of the Infinite.

'He who experiences the unity of life, sees his own Self in all beings, and all beings in his own Self, and looks on everything with an impartial eye;

'He who sees Me in everything and everything in Me, him shall I never forsake, nor shall he lose Me.

'The sage who realises the unity of life and who worships Me in all beings, lives in Me, whatever may be his lot.

'O Arjuna! He is the perfect saint who, taught by the likeness within himself, sees the same Self everywhere, whether the outer form be pleasurable or painful.'

Arjuna said: 'I do not see how I can attain this state of equanimity which Thou hast revealed, owing to the restlessness of my mind.

'My Lord! Verily, the mind is fickle and turbulent, obstinate and strong, yea extremely difficult as the wind to control.'

Lord Shri Krishna replied: 'Doubtless, O Mighty One! the mind is fickle and exceedingly difficult to restrain, but, O son of Kunti! with practice and renunciation it can be done.

'It is not possible to attain Self-Realisation if a man does not know how to control himself; but for him who, striving by proper means, learns such control, it is possible.'

Arjuna asked: 'He who fails to control himself, whose mind falls from spiritual contemplation, who attains not perfection but retains his faith, what of him, my Lord?

'Having failed in both, my Lord! is he without hope, like a riven cloud having no support, lost on the spiritual road?

'My Lord! Thou art worthy to solve this doubt once for all; save Thyself there is no one competent to do so.'

Lord Shri Krishna replied: 'My beloved child! There is no destruction for him, either in this world or in the next. No evil fate awaits him who treads the path of righteousness.

'Having reached the worlds where the righteous dwell, and having remained there for many years, he who has slipped away from the path of spirituality will be born again in the family of the pure, benevolent and prosperous.

'Or, he may be born in the family of the wise sages; though a birth like this is, indeed, very difficult to obtain.

'Then the experience acquired in his former life will revive, and with its help he will strive for perfection more eagerly than before.

'Unconsciously he will return to the practices of his old life; so that he who tries to realise spiritual consciousness is certainly superior to one who only talks of it.

'Then, after many lives, the student of spirituality who earnestly strives, and whose sins are absolved, attains perfection and reaches the Supreme.

'The wise man is superior to the ascetic and to the scholar and to the man of action; therefore be thou a wise man, O Arjuna!

'I look upon him as the best of mystics who, full of faith, worshippeth Me and abideth in Me.'

Thus, in the Holy Book the Bhagavad-Geetā, one of the Upanishads, in the Science of the Supreme Spirit, in the Art of Self-Knowledge, in the colloquy between the Divine Lord Shri Krishna and the Prince Arjuna, stands the sixth chapter, entitled: Self-Control.

CHAPTER VII

★

Lord Shri Krishna said: 'Listen, O Arjuna! And I will tell thee how thou shalt know Me in My full perfection, practising meditation with thy mind devoted to Me, and having Me for thy refuge.

'I will reveal this knowledge unto thee, and how it may be realised; which, once accomplished, there remains nothing else worth having in this life.

'Among thousands of men scarcely one strives for perfection, and even amongst those who gain occult powers, perchance but one knows Me in truth.

'Earth, water, fire, air, aether, mind, intellect and personality; this is the eightfold division of My Manifested Nature.

'This is My inferior Nature; but distinct from this, O Valiant One! know thou that my Superior Nature is the very Life which sustains the universe.

'It is the womb of all being; for I am He by Whom the worlds were created and shall be dissolved.

'O Arjuna! There is nothing higher than Me; all is strung upon Me as rows of pearls upon a thread.

'O Arjuna! I am the Fluidity in water, the Light in the sun and in the moon. I am the mystic syllable Ôm in the Vedic scriptures, the Sound in aether, the Virility in man.

'I am the Fragrance of earth, the Brilliance of fire. I am the Life-force in all beings, and I am the Austerity of the ascetics.

'Know, O Arjuna! that I am the eternal Seed of being; I am the Intelligence of the intelligent, the Splendour of the resplendent.

'I am the Strength of the strong, of them who are free from attachment and desire; and, O Arjuna! I am the Desire for righteousness.

'Whatever be the nature of their life, whether it be pure or passionate or ignorant, they all are derived from Me. They are in Me, but I am not in them.

'The inhabitants of this world, misled by those natures which the Qualities have engendered, know not that I am higher than them all, and that I do not change.

'Verily, this Divine Illusion of Phenomenon manifesting itself in the Qualities is difficult to surmount. Only they who devote themselves to Me and to Me alone can accomplish it.

'The sinner, the ignorant, the vile, deprived of spiritual perception by the glamour of Illusion, and he who pursues a godless life—none of them shall find Me.

'O Arjuna! The righteous who worship Me are grouped by stages: first they who suffer, next they who desire knowledge, then they who thirst after truth, and lastly they who attain wisdom.

'Of all these, he who has gained wisdom, who meditates on Me without ceasing, devoting himself only to Me, he is the best; for by the wise man I am exceedingly beloved and the wise man, too, is beloved by Me.

'Noble-minded are they all, but the wise man I hold as my own Self; for he, remaining always at peace with Me, makes Me his final goal.

'After many lives, at last the wise man realises Me as I am. A man so enlightened that he sees God everywhere is very difficult to find.

'They in whom wisdom is obscured by one desire or the other, worship the lesser Powers, practising many rites which vary according to their temperaments.

'But whatever the form of worship, if the devotee have faith, then upon his faith in that worship do I set My own seal.

'If he worships one form alone with real faith, then shall his desires be fulfilled through that only; for thus have I ordained.

'The fruit that comes to men of limited insight is, after all, finite. They who worship the Lower Powers attain them; but those who worship Me come unto Me alone.

'The ignorant think of Me, who am the Unmanifested Spirit, as if I were really in human form. They do not understand that My Supreme Nature is changeless and most excellent.

'I am not visible to all, for I am enveloped by the illusion of Phenomenon. This deluded world does not know Me, as the Unborn and the Imperishable.

'I know, O Arjuna! all beings in the past, the present and the future; but they do not know Me.

'O brave Arjuna! Man lives in a fairy world, deceived by the glamour of opposite sensations, infatuated by desire and aversion.

'But those who act righteously, in whom sin has been destroyed, who are free from the infatuation of the conflicting emotions, they worship Me with firm resolution.

'Those who make Me their refuge, who strive for liberation from decay and death; they realise the Supreme Spirit, which is their own real Self, and in which all action finds its consummation.

'Those who see Me in the life of the world, in the universal

49

sacrifice, and as pure Divinity, keeping their minds steady, they live in Me, even in the crucial hour of death.'

Thus, in the Holy Book the Bhagavad-Geetā, one of the Upanishads, in the Science of the Supreme Spirit, in the Art of Self-Knowledge, in the colloquy between the Divine Lord Shri Krishna and the Prince Arjuna, stands the seventh chapter, entitled: Knowledge and Experience.

CHAPTER VIII

★

Arjuna asked: 'O Lord of Lords! What is that which men call the Supreme Spirit, what is man's Spiritual Nature, and what is the Law? What is Matter and what is Divinity?

'Who is it who rules the spirit of sacrifice in man; and at the time of death how may those who have learned self-control come to the knowledge of Thee?'

The Lord Shri Krishna replied: 'The Supreme Spirit is the Highest Imperishable Self, and Its Nature is spiritual consciousness. The worlds have been created and are supported by an emanation from the Spirit which is called the Law.

'Matter consists of the forms that perish; Divinity is the Supreme Self; and He who inspires the spirit of sacrifice in man, O noblest of thy race! is I Myself, Who now stand in human form before thee.

'Whosoever at the time of death thinks only of Me, and thinking thus leaves the body and goes forth, assuredly he will know Me.

'On whatever sphere of being the mind of a man may be intent at the time of death, thither will he go.

'Therefore meditate always on Me, and fight; if thy mind and thy reason be fixed on Me, to Me shalt thou surely come.

'He whose mind does not wander, and who is engaged in constant meditation, attains the Supreme Spirit.

'Whoso meditates on the Omniscient, the Ancient, more Minute than the atom, yet the Ruler and Upholder of all,

Unimaginable, Brilliant like the Sun, Beyond the reach of darkness;

'He who leaves the body with mind unmoved and filled with devotion, by the power of his meditation gathering between his eyebrows his whole vital energy, attains the Supreme.

'Now I will speak briefly of the imperishable goal, proclaimed by those versed in the scriptures, which the mystic attains when free from passion, and for which he is content to undergo the vow of continence.

'Closing the gates of the body, drawing the forces of his mind into the heart and by the power of meditation concentrating his vital energy in the brain;

'Repeating Ôm, the Symbol of Eternity, holding Me always in remembrance, he who thus leaves his body and goes forth reaches the Spirit Supreme.

'To him who thinks constantly of Me, and of nothing else, to such an ever-faithful devotee, O Arjuna! am I ever accessible.

'Coming thus unto Me, these great souls go no more to the misery and death of earthly life, for they have gained perfection.

'The worlds, with the whole realm of creation, come and go; but, O Arjuna! whoso comes to Me, for him there is no rebirth.

'Those who understand the cosmic day and cosmic night know that one day of creation is a thousand cycles, and that the night is of equal length.

'At the dawning of that day all objects in manifestation stream forth from the Unmanifest, and when evening falls they are dissolved into It again.

'The same multitude of beings, which have lived on earth so often, all are dissolved as the night of the universe approaches, to issue forth anew when morning breaks. Thus is it ordained.

'In truth, therefore, there is the Eternal Unmanifest, which is beyond and above the Unmanifest Spirit of Creation, which is never destroyed when all these beings perish.

'The wise say that the Unmanifest and Indestructible is the highest goal of all; when once That is reached, there is no return. That is My Blessed Home.

'O Arjuna! That Highest God, in Whom all beings abide, and Who pervades the entire universe, is reached only by whole-hearted devotion.

'Now I will tell thee, O Arjuna! of the times at which, if the mystics go forth, they do not return, and at which they go forth only to return.

'If knowing the Supreme Spirit the sage goes forth with fire and light, in the daytime, in the fortnight of the waxing moon, and in the six months before the Northern summer solstice, he will attain the Supreme.

'But if he departs in gloom, at night, during the fortnight of the waning moon and in the six months before the Southern solstice, then he reaches but lunar light and he will be born again.

'These bright and dark paths out of the world have always existed. Whoso takes the former, returns not; he who chooses the latter, returns.

'O Arjuna! The saint knowing these paths is not confused. Therefore meditate perpetually.

'The sage who knows this passes beyond all merit that comes from the study of the scriptures, from sacrifice, from austerities and charity, and reaches the Supreme Primeval Abode.'

Thus, in the Holy Book the Bhagavad-Geetā, one of the Upanishads, in the Science of the Supreme Spirit, in the Art of Self-Knowledge, in the colloquy between the Divine Lord Shri Krishna and the Prince Arjuna, stands the eighth chapter, entitled: The Life Everlasting.

CHAPTER IX

★

Lord Shri Krishna said: 'I will now reveal to thee, since thou doubtest not, that profound mysticism, which when followed by experience, shall liberate thee from sin.

'This is the Premier Science, the Sovereign Secret, the Purest and Best; intuitional, righteous; and to him who practiseth it pleasant beyond measure.

'They who have no faith in this teaching cannot find Me, but remain lost in the purlieus of this perishable world.

'The whole world is pervaded by Me, yet My form is not seen. All living things have their being in Me, yet I am not limited by them.

'Nevertheless, they do not consciously abide in Me. Such is My Divine Sovereignty that though I, the Supreme Self, am the cause and upholder of all, yet I remain outside.

'As the mighty wind, though moving everywhere, has no resting place but space, so have all these beings no home but Me.

'All beings, O Arjuna! return at the close of every cosmic cycle into the realm of Nature, which is a part of Me, and at the beginning of the next I send them forth again.

'With the help of Nature, again and again I pour forth the whole multitude of beings, whether they will or no, for they are ruled by My Will.

'But these acts of Mine do not bind Me. I remain outside and unattached.

'Under My guidance, Nature produces all things movable and immovable. Thus it is, O Arjuna! that this universe revolves.

'Fools disregard Me, seeing Me clad in human form. They know not that in My higher nature I am the Lord-God of all.

'Their hopes are vain, their actions worthless, their knowledge futile, they are without sense, deceitful, barbarous and godless.

'But the Great Souls, O Arjuna! filled with My Divine Spirit, they worship Me, they fix their minds on Me and on Me alone, for they know that I am the imperishable Source of being.

'Always extolling Me, strenuous, firm in their vows, prostrating themselves before Me, they worship Me continually with concentrated devotion.

'Others worship Me with full consciousness, as the One, the Manifold, the Omnipresent, the Universal.

'I am the Oblation, the Sacrifice, and the Worship; I am the Fuel and the Chant, I am the Butter offered to the fire, I am the Fire itself; and I am the Act of offering.

'I am the Father of the universe and its Mother; I am its Nourisher and its Grandfather; I am the Knowable and the Pure; I am Ôm; and I am the Sacred Scriptures.

'I am the Goal, the Sustainer, the Lord, the Witness, the Home, the Shelter, the Lover and the Origin; I am Life and Death; I am the Fountain and the Seed Imperishable.

'I am the Heat of the Sun. I release and hold back the Rains. I am Death and Immortality; I am Being and Not-Being.

'Those who are versed in the scriptures, who drink the mystic Sôma-juice and are purified from sin, but who while worshipping Me with sacrifices pray that I will lead them to heaven; they reach the holy world where lives the Controller of the Powers of Nature, and they enjoy the feasts of Paradise.

'Yet although they enjoy the spacious glories of Paradise, nevertheless, when their merit is exhausted, they are born again into this world of mortals. They have followed the letter of the scriptures, yet because they have sought but to fulfil their own desires, they must depart and return again and again.

'But if a man will meditate on Me and Me alone, and will worship Me always and everywhere, I will take upon Myself the fulfilment of his aspiration, and I will safeguard whatsoever he shall attain.

'Even those who worship the lesser Powers, if they do so with faith, they thereby worship Me, though not in the right way.

'I am the willing recipient of sacrifice, and I am its true Lord. But these do not know Me in truth, and so they sink back.

'The votaries of the lesser Powers go to them; the devotees of spirits go to them; they who worship the Powers of Darkness, to such Powers shall they go; and so, too, those who worship Me shall come unto Me.

'Whatever a man offers to Me, whether it be a leaf, or a flower, or fruit, or water, I accept it, for it is offered with devotion and purity of mind.

'Whatever thou doest, whatever thou dost eat, whatever thou dost sacrifice and give, whatever austerities thou practisest, do all as an offering to Me.

'So shall thy action be attended by no result, either good or bad; but through the spirit of renunciation thou shalt come to Me and be free.

'I am the same to all beings. I favour none, and I hate none. But those who worship Me devotedly, they live in Me, and I in them.

'Even the most sinful, if he worship Me with his whole heart, shall be considered righteous, for he is treading the right path.

'He shall attain spirituality ere long, and Eternal Peace shall be his. O Arjuna! Believe me, My devotee is never lost.

'For even the children of sinful parents, and those mis-called the weaker sex, and merchants, and labourers, if only they will make Me their refuge, they shall attain the Highest.

'What need then to mention the holy Ministers of God, the devotees and the saintly rulers? Do thou, therefore, born in this changing and miserable world, do thou too worship Me.

'Fix thy mind on Me, devote thyself to Me, sacrifice for Me, surrender to Me, make Me the object of thy aspirations, and thou shalt assuredly become one with Me, Who am thine own Self.'

Thus, in the Holy Book the Bhagavad-Geetā, one of the Upanishads, in the Science of the Supreme Spirit, in the Art of Self-Knowledge, in the colloquy between the Divine Lord Shri Krishna and the Prince Arjuna, stands the ninth chapter, entitled: The Science of Sciences and The Mystery of Mysteries.

CHAPTER X

★

Lord Shri Krishna said: 'Now, O Prince! Listen to My supreme advice, which I give thee for the sake of thy welfare, for thou art My beloved.

'Neither the professors of divinity, nor the great ascetics know My origin, for I am the source of them all.

'He who knows Me as the unborn, without beginning, the Lord of the universe, he, stripped of his delusions, becomes free from all conceivable sin.

'Intelligence, wisdom, non-illusion, forgiveness, truth, self-control, calmness, pleasure, pain, birth, death, fear and fearlessness;

'Harmlessness, equanimity, contentment, austerity, beneficence, fame and failure, all these, the characteristics of beings, spring from Me only.

'The seven Great Seers,[1] the Progenitors of mankind, the Ancient Four,[2] and the Lawgivers, were born of My Will and came forth direct from Me. The race of mankind has sprung from them.

'He who rightly understands My manifested glory and My Creative Power, beyond doubt attains perfect Peace.

'I am the source of all; from Me everything flows. Therefore the wise worship Me with unchanging devotion.

[1] Mareechi, Atri, Angirā, Pulah, Kratu, Pulastya, Vashishtha.
[2] The Masters, Sanak, Sanandan, Sanātan, Sanatkumār.

'With minds concentrated on Me, with lives absorbed in Me, and enlightening each other, they ever feel content and happy.

'To those who are always devout and who worship Me with love, I give the power of discrimination, which leads them to Me.

'By My grace, I live in their hearts; and I dispel the darkness of ignorance by the shining light of wisdom.'

Arjuna asked: 'Thou art the Supreme Spirit, the Eternal Home, the Holiest of the Holy, the Eternal Divine Self, the Primal God, the Unborn, and the Omnipresent.

'So have said the seers and the divine sage Nārada; as well as Asita, Devala and Vyāsa; and Thou Thyself also sayest it.

'I believe in what Thou hast said, my Lord! For neither the godly nor the godless comprehend Thy manifestation.

'Thou alone knowest Thyself, by the power of Thy Self; Thou the Supreme Spirit, the Source and Master of all being, the Lord of Lords, the Ruler of the Universe.

'Please tell me all about Thy glorious manifestations, by means of which Thou pervadest the world.

'O Master! How shall I, by constant meditation, know Thee? My Lord! What are Thy various manifestations through which I am to meditate on Thee?

'Tell me again, I pray, about the fullness of Thy power and Thy glory; for I feel that I am never satisfied when I listen to Thy immortal words.'

Lord Shri Krishna replied: 'So be it, My beloved friend! I will unfold to thee some of the chief aspects of My glory. Of its full extent there is no end.

'O Arjuna! I am the Self, seated in the hearts of all beings; I am the beginning and the life, and I am the end of them all.

'Of all creative Powers I am the Creator, of luminaries the Sun; the Whirlwind among the winds, and the Moon among planets.

'Of the Vedās I am the Hymns, I am the Electric Force in the Powers of Nature; of the senses I am the Mind; and I am the Intelligence in all that lives.

'Among Forces of Vitality I am the Life, I am Mammon to the heathen and the godless; I am the Energy in fire, earth, wind, sky, heaven, sun, moon and planets; and among mountains I am the Mount Meru.

'Among the priests, know, O Arjuna! that I am the Apostle Brihaspati, of generals I am Skanda the Commander-in-Chief, and of waters I am the Ocean.

'Of the great seers I am Bhrigu, of words I am Ôm, of offerings I am the silent prayer, among things immovable I am the Himālayās.

'Of trees I am the sacred Fig-tree, of the Divine Seers Nārada, of the heavenly singers I am Chitraratha, their Leader, and of sages I am Kapila.

'Know that among horses I am Pegasus, the heaven-born; among the lordly elephants I am the White one, and I am the Ruler among men.

'I am the Thunderbolt among weapons; of cows I am the Cow of Plenty, I am Passion in those who procreate, and I am the Cobra among serpents.

'I am the King-python among snakes, I am the Aqueous Principle among those that live in water, I am the Father of fathers, and among rulers I am Death.

'And I am the devotee Prahlād among the heathen; of Time I am the Eternal Present; I am the Lion among beasts, and the Eagle among birds.

'I am the Wind among the purifiers, the King Rāma among warriors, I am the Crocodile among the fishes, and I am the Ganges among the rivers.

'I am the Beginning, the Middle and the End in creation; among sciences, I am the science of Spirituality; I am the Discussion amongst disputants.

'Of letters I am A; I am the copulative in compound words; I am Time inexhaustible; and I am the all-pervading Preserver.

'I am all-devouring Death; I am the Origin of all that shall happen; I am Fame, Fortune, Speech, Memory, Intellect, Constancy and Forgiveness.

'Of hymns I am Brihatsāma, of metres I am Gāyatri, among the months I am Mārgasheersha (December), and I am the Spring among seasons.

'I am the Gambling of the cheat, and the Splendour of the splendid; I am Victory; I am Effort; and I am the Purity of the pure.

'I am Shri Krishna among the Vrishni-clan, and Arjuna among the Pāndavās; of the saints I am Vyāsa, and I am the Shukrāchārya among the sages.

'I am the Sceptre of rulers, the Strategy of the conquerors, the Silence of mystery, the Wisdom of the wise.

'I am the Seed of all being, O Arjuna! No creature moving or unmoving can live without Me.

'O Arjuna! The aspects of My divine life are endless. I have mentioned but a few by way of illustration.

'Whatever is glorious, excellent, beautiful and mighty, be assured that it comes from a fragment of My splendour.

'But what is the use of all these details to thee? O Arjuna! I sustain this universe with only a small part of Myself.'

Thus, in the Holy Book the Bhagavad-Geetā, one of the Upanishads, in the Science of the Supreme Spirit, in the Art of Self-Knowledge, in the colloquy between the Divine Lord Shri Krishna and the Prince Arjuna, stands the tenth chapter, entitled: The Divine Manifestations.

CHAPTER XI

★

Arjuna said: 'My Lord! Thy words concerning the Supreme Secret of Self, given for my blessing, have dispelled the illusions which surrounded me.

'O Lord! Whose eyes are like the lotus-petal! Thou hast described in detail the origin and the dissolution of being, and Thine own Eternal Majesty.

'I believe all as Thou hast declared it. I long now to have a vision of Thy Divine Form, O Thou Most High!

'If Thou thinkest that it can be made possible for me to see it, show me, O Lord of Lords! Thine own Eternal Self.'

Lord Shri Krishna replied: 'Behold, O Arjuna! My celestial forms, by hundreds and thousands, various in kind, in colour and in shape.

'Behold thou the Powers of Nature: fire, earth, wind and sky; the sun, the heavens, the moon, the stars; all the forces of vitality and of healing; and the roving winds. See the myriad wonders revealed to none but thee.

'Here, in Me living as one, O Arjuna! behold the whole universe, movable and immovable, and anything else that thou wouldst see.

'Yet since with mortal eyes thou canst not see Me, lo! I give thee the Divine Sight. See now the glory of My Sovereignty.'

Sanjaya continued: Having thus spoken, O King! The Lord Shri Krishna, the Almighty Prince of Wisdom, showed to Arjuna the Supreme Form of the Great God.

There were countless eyes and mouths, and mystic forms innumerable, with shining ornaments and flaming celestial weapons.

Crowned with heavenly garlands, clothed in shining garments, anointed with divine unctions, He showed Himself as the Resplendent One, Marvellous, Boundless, Omnipresent.

Could a thousand suns blaze forth together it would be but a faint reflection of the radiance of the Lord-God.

In that vision Arjuna saw the universe, with its manifold shapes, all embraced in One, its Supreme Lord.

Thereupon Arjuna, dumb with awe, his hair on end, his head bowed, his hands clasped in salutation, addressed the Lord thus:

Arjuna said: 'O Almighty God! I see in Thee the powers of Nature, the various creatures of the world, the Progenitor on his lotus-throne, the Sages and the shining angels.

'I see Thee, infinite in form, with as it were, faces, eyes and limbs everywhere; no beginning, no middle, no end; O Thou Lord of the Universe, Whose Form is universal!

'I see Thee with the crown, the sceptre and the discus; a blaze of splendour. Scarce can I gaze on Thee, so radiant Thou art, glowing like the blazing fire, brilliant as the sun, immeasurable.

'Imperishable art Thou, the Sole One worthy to be known, the priceless Treasure-house of the universe, the immortal Guardian of the Life Eternal, the Spirit Everlasting.

'Without beginning, without middle and without end, infinite in power, Thine arms all-embracing, the sun and moon Thine eyes, Thy face beaming with the fire of sacrifice, flooding the whole universe with light.

'Alone Thou fillest all the quarters of the sky, earth and heaven, and the regions between. O Almighty Lord! Seeing

Thy marvellous and awe-inspiring Form, the spheres tremble with fear.

'The troops of celestial Beings enter into Thee, some invoking Thee in fear, with folded palms; the Great Seers and Adepts sing hymns to Thy Glory, saying "All Hail".

'The Vital Forces, the Major stars, Fire, Earth, Air, Sky, Sun, Heaven, Moon and Planets; the Angels, the Guardians of the Universe, the divine Healers, the Winds, the Fathers, the Heavenly Singers; and hosts of Mammon-worshippers, demons as well as saints, are amazed.

'Seeing Thy stupendous Form, O Most Mighty! with its myriad faces, its innumerable eyes and limbs and terrible jaws, I myself and all the worlds are overwhelmed with awe.

'When I see Thee, touching the Heavens, glowing with colour, with open mouth and wide open fiery eyes, I am terrified. O my Lord! my courage and my peace of mind desert me.

'When I see Thy mouths with their fearful jaws like glowing fires at the dissolution of creation, I lose all sense of place; I find no rest. Be merciful, O Lord in whom this universe abides!

'All these sons of Dhritarāshtra, with the hosts of princes, Bheeshma, Drôna and Karna, as well as the other warrior chiefs belonging to our side;

'I see them all rushing headlong into Thy mouths, with terrible tusks, horrible to behold. Some are mangled between Thy jaws, with their heads crushed to atoms.

'As rivers in flood surge furiously to the ocean, so these heroes; the greatest among men, fling themselves into Thy flaming mouths.

'As moths fly impetuously to the flame only to be killed, so these men rush into Thy mouths to court their own destruction.

'Thou seemest to swallow up the worlds, to lap them in flame. Thy glory fills the universe. Thy fierce rays beat down upon it irresistibly.

'Tell me then who Thou art, that wearest this dreadful Form? I bow before Thee, O Mighty One! Have mercy, I pray, and let me see Thee as Thou wert at first. I do not know what Thou intendest.'

Lord Shri Krishna replied: 'I have shown myself to thee as the Destroyer who lays waste the world, and whose purpose now is destruction. In spite of thy efforts, all these warriors gathered for battle shall not escape death.

'Then gird up thy loins, and conquer. Subdue thy foes and enjoy the kingdom in prosperity. I have already doomed them. Be thou my instrument, Arjuna!

'Drôna and Bheeshma, Jayadratha and Karna, and other brave warriors—I have condemned them all. Destroy them; fight and fear not. Thy foes shall be crushed.'

Sanjaya continued: Having heard these words from the Lord Shri Krishna, the Prince Arjuna, with folded hands trembling, prostrated himself and with choking voice, bowing down again and again, and overwhelmed with awe, once more addressed the Lord.

Arjuna said: 'My Lord! It is natural that the world revels and rejoices when it sings the praises of Thy glory; the demons fly in fear and the saints offer Thee their salutations.

'How should they do otherwise? O Thou Supremest Self, greater than the Powers of creation, the First Cause, Infinite, the Lord of Lords, the Home of the universe, Imperishable, Being and Not-Being, yet transcending both.

'Thou art the Primal God, the Ancient, the Supreme Abode of this universe, the Knower, the Knowledge and the Final Home. Thou fillest everything. Thy form is infinite.

66

'Thou art the Wind, Thou art Death, Thou art the Fire, the Water, the Moon, the Father and the Grandfather. Honour and glory to Thee a thousand and a thousand times! Again and again, salutation be to Thee, O my Lord!

'Salutations to Thee in front and on every side, Thou who encompasseth me round about. Thy power is infinite; Thy majesty immeasurable; Thou upholdest all things; yea, Thou Thyself art All.

'Whatever I have said unto Thee in rashness, taking Thee only for a friend and addressing Thee as "O Krishna! O Yādava! O Friend!" in thoughtless familiarity, not understanding Thy greatness;

'Whatever insult I have offered to Thee in jest, in sport or in repose, in conversation or at the banquet, alone or in a multitude, I ask Thy forgiveness for them all, O Thou Who art without an equal!

'For Thou art the Father of all things movable and immovable, the Worshipful, the Master of Masters! In all the worlds there is none equal to Thee; how then superior; O Thou who standeth alone, Supreme.

'Therefore I prostrate myself before Thee, O Lord! Most Adorable! I salute Thee, I ask Thy blessing. Only Thou canst be trusted to bear with me, as father to son, as friend to friend, as lover to his beloved.

'I rejoice that I have seen what never man saw before; yet, O Lord! I am overwhelmed with fear. Please take again the Form I know. Be merciful, O Lord! Thou Who art the Home of the whole universe.

'I long to see Thee as Thou wert before, with the crown, the sceptre and the discus in Thy hands; in Thy other Form, with Thy four hands, O Thou Whose arms are countless and Whose forms are infinite.'

Lord Shri Krishna replied: 'My beloved friend! It is only through My grace and power that thou hast been able to see this vision of splendour, the Universal, the Infinite, the Original. Never has it been seen by any but thee.

'Not by study of the scriptures, not by sacrifice or gift, not by ritual or rigorous austerity, is it possible for man on earth to see what thou hast seen, O thou foremost hero of the Kuru-clan!

'Be not afraid, or bewildered, by the terrible vision. Put away thy fear and, with joyful mind, see Me once again in My usual Form.'

Sanjaya continued: Having thus spoken to Arjuna, Lord Shri Krishna showed Himself again in His accustomed form; and the Mighty Lord, in gentle tones, softly consoled him who lately trembled with fear.

Arjuna said: 'Seeing Thee in Thy gentle human form, my Lord, I am myself again, calm once more.'

Lord Shri Krishna replied: 'It is hard to see this vision of Me that thou hast seen. Even the most powerful have longed for it in vain.

'Not by study of the scriptures, or by austerities, not by gifts or sacrifices, is it possible to see Me as thou hast done.

'Only by tireless devotion can I be seen and known; only thus can a man become one with Me, O Arjuna!

'He whose every action is done for My sake, to whom I am the final goal, who loves Me only and hates no one—O My dearest Son! Only he can realise Me.'

Thus, in the Holy Book the Bhagavad-Geetā, one of the Upanishads, in the Science of the Supreme Spirit, in the Art of Self-Knowledge, in the colloquy between the Divine Lord Shri Krishna and the Prince Arjuna, stands the eleventh chapter, entitled: The Cosmic Vision.

CHAPTER XII

★

Arjuna asked: 'My Lord! Which are the better devotees who worship Thee, those who try to know Thee as a Personal God, or those who worship Thee as Impersonal and Indestructible?'

Lord Shri Krishna replied: 'Those who keep their minds fixed on Me, who worship Me always with unwavering faith and concentration; these are the very best.

'Those who worship Me as the Indestructible, the Undefinable, the Unmanifest, the Omnipresent, the Unthinkable, the Primeval, the Immutable and the Eternal;

'Subduing their senses, viewing all conditions of life with the same eye, and working for the welfare of all beings, assuredly they come to Me.

'But they who thus fix their attention on the Absolute and Impersonal encounter greater hardships; for it is difficult for those who possess a body to realise Me as without one.

'Verily, those who surrender their actions to Me, who muse on Me, worship Me and meditate on Me alone, with no thought save of Me,

'O Arjuna! I rescue them quickly from the ocean of life and death, for their minds are fixed on Me.

'Then let thy mind cling only to Me, let thy intellect abide in Me; and without doubt thou shalt live hereafter in Me alone.

'But if thou canst not fix thy mind firmly on Me, then, My beloved friend! try to do so by constant practice.

69

'And if thou art not strong enough to practise concentration, then devote thyself to My service, do all thine acts for My sake, and thou shalt still attain the goal.

'And if thou art too weak even for this, then seek refuge in union with Me, and with perfect self-control renounce the fruit of all thy action.

'Knowledge is superior to blind action, meditation to mere knowledge, renunciation of the fruit of action to meditation, and where there is renunciation peace will follow.

'He who is incapable of hatred towards any being, who is kind and compassionate, free from selfishness, without pride, equable in pleasure and in pain, and forgiving,

'Always contented, self-centred, self-controlled, resolute, with mind and reason dedicated to Me, such a devotee of Mine is My beloved.

'He who does not harm the world, and whom the world cannot harm, who is not carried away by any impulse of joy, anger or fear, such an one is My beloved.

'He who expects nothing, who is pure, watchful, indifferent, unruffled, and who renounces all initiative, such an one is My beloved.

'He who is beyond joy and hate, who neither laments nor desires, to whom good and evil fortunes are the same, such an one is My beloved.

'He to whom friend and foe are alike, who welcomes equally honour and dishonour, heat and cold, pleasure and pain, who is enamoured of nothing,

'Who is indifferent to praise and censure, who enjoys silence, who is contented with every fate, who has no fixed abode, who is steadfast in mind, and filled with devotion, such an one is My beloved.

'Verily those who love the spiritual wisdom as I have taught, whose faith never fails, and who concentrate

their whole nature on Me, they indeed are My most beloved.'

Thus, in the Holy Book the Bhagavad-Geetā, one of the
Upanishads, in the Science of the Supreme Spirit, in the
Art of Self-Knowledge, in the colloquy between the Divine
Lord Shri Krishna and the Prince Arjuna, stands the
twelfth chapter, entitled: Bhakti-Yôga or The Path of
Love.

CHAPTER XIII

★

Arjuna asked: 'My Lord! Who is God and what is Nature; what is Matter and what is the Self; what is that they call Wisdom, and what is it that is worth knowing? I wish to have this explained.'

Lord Shri Krishna replied: 'O Arjuna! The body of man is the playground of the Self; and That which knows the activities of Matter, sages call the Self.

'I am the Omniscient Self that abides in the playground of Matter; knowledge of Matter and of the all-knowing Self is wisdom.

'What is called Matter, of what it is composed, whence it came, and why it changes, what the Self is, and what Its power—this I will now briefly set forth.

'Seers have sung of It in various ways, in many hymns and sacred Vedic songs, weighty in thought, and convincing in argument.

'The five great fundamentals (earth, fire, air, water and aether), personality, intellect, the mysterious life-force, the ten organs of perception and action, the mind and the five domains of sensation;

'Desire, aversion, pleasure, pain, sympathy, vitality, and the persistent clinging to life, these are in brief the constituents of changing Matter.

'Humility, sincerity, harmlessness, forgiveness, rectitude, service of the Master, purity, steadfastness, self-control;

'Renunciation of the delights of sense, absence of pride,

right understanding of the painful problems of birth and death, of age and sickness;

'Indifference, non-attachment to sex, progeny or home, equanimity in good fortune and in bad;

'Unswerving devotion to Me, by concentration on Me and Me alone, a love for solitude, indifference to social life;

'Constant yearning for the knowledge of Self, and pondering over the lessons of the great Truth—this is Wisdom, all else ignorance.

'I will speak to thee now of that great Truth which man ought to know, since by its means he will win immortal bliss; That which is without beginning, the Eternal Spirit which dwells in Me, neither with form, nor yet without it.

'Everywhere are Its hands and Its feet, everywhere It has eyes that see, heads that think, and mouths that speak; everywhere It listens; It dwells in all the worlds; It envelops them all.

'Beyond the senses, It yet shines through every sense-perception. Bound to nothing, It yet sustains everything. Unaffected by the Qualities, It still enjoys them all.

'It is within all beings, yet outside; motionless yet moving; too subtle to be perceived; far away yet always near.

'In all beings undivided, yet living in division, It is the upholder of all, Creator and Destroyer alike;

'It is the Light of lights, beyond the reach of darkness; the Wisdom, the only thing that is worth knowing or that wisdom can teach; the Presence in the hearts of all.

'Thus have I told thee in brief what Matter is, and the Self worth realising and what is Wisdom. He who is devoted to Me knows; and assuredly he will enter into Me.

'Know thou further that Nature and God have no beginning; and that differences of character and quality have their origin in Nature only.

'Nature is the Law which generates cause and effect; God is the source of the enjoyment of all pleasure and pain.

'God dwelling in the heart of Nature experiences the Qualities which Nature brings forth; and His affinity towards the Qualities is the reason for His living in a good or evil body.

'Thus in the body of man dwells the Supreme God; He who sees and permits, upholds and enjoys; the Highest God and the Highest Self.

'He who understands God and Nature along with her Qualities, whatever be his condition in life, he comes not again to earth.

'Some realise the Supreme by meditating, by Its aid, on the Self within, others by pure reason, others by right action.

'Others again, having no direct knowledge but only hearing from others, nevertheless worship, and they too, if true to the teachings, cross the sea of death.

'Wherever life is seen in things movable or immovable, it is the joint product of Matter and Spirit.

'He who can see the Supreme Lord in all beings, the Imperishable amidst the perishable, he it is who really sees.

'Beholding the Lord in all things equally, his actions do not mar his spiritual life but lead him to the height of Bliss.

'He who understands that it is only Law of Nature that brings action to fruition, and that the Self never acts, alone knows the Truth.

'He who sees the diverse forms of life all rooted in the One, and growing forth from Him, he shall indeed find the Absolute.

'The Supreme Spirit, O Prince! is without beginning, without Qualities and Imperishable, and though it be within the body, yet It does not act, nor is It affected by action.

'As space, though present everywhere, remains by reason

of its subtlety unaffected, so the Self, though present in all forms, retains its purity unalloyed.

'As the one Sun illuminates the whole earth, so the Lord illumines the whole universe.

'Those who with the eyes of wisdom thus see the difference between Matter and Spirit, and know how to liberate Life from the Law of Nature, they attain the Supreme.'

Thus, in the Holy Book the Bhagavad-Geetā, one of the Upanishads, in the Science of the Supreme Spirit, in the Art of Self-Knowledge, in the colloquy between the Divine Lord Shri Krishna and the Prince Arjuna, stands the thirteenth chapter, entitled: Spirit and Matter.

CHAPTER XIV

★

Lord Shri Krishna continued: 'Now I will reveal unto thee the Wisdom which is beyond knowledge, by attaining which the sages have reached Perfection.

'Dwelling in Wisdom and realising My Divinity, they are not born again when the universe is recreated at the beginning of every cycle, nor are they affected when it is dissolved.

'The eternal Cosmos is My womb, in which I plant the seed, from which all beings are born, O Prince!

'O illustrious son of Kunti! Through whatever wombs men are born, it is the Spirit Itself that conceives, and I am their Father.

'Purity, Passion and Ignorance are the Qualities which the Law of Nature bringeth forth. They fetter the free Spirit in all beings.

'O Sinless One! Of these, Purity, being luminous, strong and invulnerable, binds one by its yearning for happiness and illumination.

'Passion, engendered by thirst for pleasure and attachment, binds the soul through its fondness for activity.

'But Ignorance, the product of darkness, stupefies the senses in all embodied beings, binding them by the chains of folly, indolence and lethargy.

'Purity brings happiness, Passion commotion, and Ignorance, which obscures wisdom, leads to a life of failure.

'O Prince! Purity prevails when Passion and Ignorance are overcome; Passion, when Purity and Ignorance are overcome; and Ignorance when it overcomes Purity and Passion.

'When the light of knowledge gleams forth from all the gates of the body, then be sure that Purity prevails.

'O best of Indians! Avarice, the impulse to act, and the beginning of action itself, are all due to the dominance of Passion.

'Darkness, stagnation, folly and infatuation are the result of the domination of Ignorance, O joy of the Kuru-clan!

'When Purity prevails, the soul on quitting the body passes on to the pure regions where live those who know the Highest.

'When Passion prevails, the soul is reborn among those who love activity; when Ignorance rules, it enters the wombs of the ignorant.

'They say the fruit of a meritorious action is spotless and full of Purity; the outcome of Passion is misery, and of Ignorance darkness.

'Purity engenders Wisdom, Passion avarice, and Ignorance folly, infatuation and darkness.

'When Purity is in the ascendant, the man evolves; when Passion, he neither evolves nor degenerates; when Ignorance, he is lost.

'As soon as a man understands that it is only the Qualities which act and nothing else, and perceives That which is beyond, he attains My divine nature.

'When the soul transcends the Qualities, which are the real cause of physical existence, then, freed from birth and death, from old age and misery, he quaffs the nectar of immortality.'

Arjuna asked: 'My Lord! By what signs can he who has

transcended the Qualities be recognised? How does he act? How does he live beyond them?'

Lord Shri Krishna replied: 'O Prince! He who shuns not the Quality which is present, and longs not for that which is absent;

'He who maintains an attitude of indifference, who is not disturbed by the Qualities, who realises that it is only they who act, and remains calm;

'Who accepts pleasure or pain as it comes, is centred in his Self, to whom a piece of clay or a stone or gold are the same, who neither likes nor dislikes, who is steadfast, indifferent alike to praise or censure;

'Who looks equally upon honour and dishonour, loves friends and foes alike, abandons all initiative, such is he who transcends the Qualities.

'And he who serves Me and only Me, with unfaltering devotion, shall overcome the Qualities, and become One with the Eternal.

'For I am the Home of the Spirit, the continual Source of immortality, of eternal Righteousness and of infinite Joy.'

Thus, in the Holy Book the Bhagavad-Geetā, one of the Upanishads, in the Science of the Supreme Spirit, in the Art of Self-Knowledge, in the colloquy between the Divine Lord Shri Krishna and the Prince Arjuna, stands the fourteenth chapter, entitled: The Three Qualities.

CHAPTER XV

★

Lord Shri Krishna continued: 'This phenomenal creation, which is both ephemeral and eternal, is like a tree, but having its seed above in the Highest, and its ramifications on this earth below. The scriptures are its leaves, and he who understands this, knows.

'Its branches shoot upwards and downwards, deriving their nourishment from the Qualities; its buds are the objects of sense; and its roots, which follow the Law causing man's regeneration and degeneration, pierce downwards into the soil.

'In this world its true form is not known, neither its origin nor its end, and its strength is not understood, until the tree with its roots striking deep into the earth is hewn down by the sharp axe of non-attachment.

'Beyond lies the Path, from which, when found, there is no return. This is the Primal God from whence this ancient creation has sprung.

'The wise attain Eternity when, freed from pride and delusion, they have conquered their love for the things of sense; when, renouncing desire and fixing their gaze on the Self, they have ceased to be tossed to and fro by the opposing sensations, like pleasure and pain.

'Neither sun, moon, nor fire shine there. Those who go thither never come back. For, O Arjuna! that is My Celestial Home.

'It is only a very small part of My Eternal Self, which is the life of this universe, drawing round itself the six senses, the mind the last, which have their source in Nature.

'When the Supreme Lord enters a body or leaves it, He gathers these senses together and travels on with them, as the wind gathers perfume while passing through the flowers.

'He is the perception of the ear, the eye, the touch, the taste and the smell, yea and of the mind also; and the enjoyment of the things which they perceive is also His.

'The ignorant do not see that it is He Who is present in life and Who departs at death or even that it is He Who enjoys pleasure through the Qualities. Only the eye of wisdom sees.

'The saints with great effort find Him within themselves; but not the unintelligent, who in spite of every effort cannot control their minds.

'Remember that the Light which, proceeding from the sun, illumines the whole world, and the Light which is in the moon, and That which is in the fire also, all are born of Me.

'I enter this world and animate all My creatures with My vitality; and by My cool moonbeams I nourish the plants.

'Becoming the fire of life, I pass into their bodies and, uniting with the vital streams of Prāna and Apāna, I digest the various kinds of food.

'I am enthroned in the hearts of all; memory, wisdom and discrimination owe their origin to Me. I am He Who is to be realised in the scriptures; I inspire their wisdom and I know their truth.

'There are two aspects in Nature: the perishable and the imperishable. All life in this world belongs to the former, the unchanging element belongs to the latter.

'But higher than all am I, the Supreme God, the Absolute

Self, the Eternal Lord, Who pervades the worlds and upholds them all.

'Beyond comparison of the Eternal with the non-eternal am I, Who am called by scriptures and sages the Supreme Personality, the Highest God.

'He who with unclouded vision sees Me as the Lord-God, knows all there is to be known, and always shall worship Me with his whole heart.

'Thus, O Sinless One! I have revealed to thee this most mystic knowledge. He who understands gains wisdom, and attains the consummation of life.'

Thus, in the Holy Book the Bhagavad-Geetā, one of the Upanishads, in the Science of the Supreme Spirit, in the Art of Self-Knowledge, in the colloquy between the Divine Lord Shri Krishna and the Prince Arjuna, stands the fifteenth chapter, entitled: The Lord-God.

CHAPTER XVI

★

Lord Shri Krishna continued: 'Fearlessness, clean living, unceasing concentration on wisdom, readiness to give, self-control, a spirit of sacrifice, regular study of the scriptures, austerities, candour,

'Harmlessness, truth, absence of wrath, renunciation, contentment, straightforwardness, compassion towards all, uncovetousness, courtesy, modesty, constancy,

'Valour, forgiveness, fortitude, purity, freedom from hate and vanity; these are his who possesses the Godly Qualities, O Arjuna!

'Hypocrisy, pride, insolence, cruelty, ignorance, belong to him who is born of the godless qualities.

'Godly qualities lead to liberation; godless to bondage. Do not be anxious, Prince! Thou hast the Godly qualities.

'All beings are of two classes: Godly and godless. The Godly I have described; I will now describe the other.

'The godless do not know how to act, or how to renounce. They have neither purity nor truth. They do not understand the right principles of conduct.

'They say that the universe is an accident with no purpose and no God. Life is created by sexual union, a product of lust and nothing else.

'Thinking thus, these degraded souls, these enemies of mankind—whose intelligence is negligible and whose deeds are monstrous—come into the world only to destroy.

'Giving themselves up to insatiable passions, hypocritical, self-sufficient and arrogant, cherishing false conceptions founded on delusion, they work only to carry out their own unholy purposes.

'Poring anxiously over evil resolutions, which only end in death; seeking only the gratification of desire as the highest goal; seeing nothing beyond;

'Caught in the toils of a hundred vain hopes, the slaves of passion and of wrath, they accumulate hoards of unjust wealth, only to pander to their sensual desire.

'This have I gained to-day, to-morrow I will gratify another desire; this wealth is mine now, the rest shall be mine ere long;

'I have slain one enemy, I will slay the others also; I am worthy to enjoy, I am the Almighty, I am perfect, powerful and happy;

'I am rich, I am well-bred; who is there to compare with me? I will sacrifice, I will give, I will pay—and I will enjoy. Thus blinded by ignorance;

'Perplexed by discordant thoughts, entangled in the snares of desire, infatuated by passion, they sink into the horrors of hell.

'Self-conceited, stubborn, rich, proud and insolent, they make a display of their patronage, disregarding the rules of decency.

'Puffed up by power and inordinate conceit, swayed by lust and wrath, these wicked people hate Me Who am within them, as I am within all.

'Those who thus hate Me, who are cruel, the dregs of man-kind, I condemn them to a continuous, miserable and god-less rebirth.

'So reborn, they spend life after life, enveloped in delusion. And they never reach Me, O Prince! but degenerate into still lower forms of life.

'The gates of hell are three: lust, wrath and avarice. They destroy the Self. Avoid them.

'These are the gates which lead to darkness; if a man avoids them he will ensure his own welfare, and in the end will attain his liberation.

'But he who neglects the commands of the scriptures, and follows the promptings of passion, he does not attain perfection, happiness, or the final goal.

'Therefore whenever there is a doubt whether thou shouldst do a thing or not, let the scriptures guide thy conduct. In the light of the scriptures shouldst thou labour the whole of thy life.'

Thus, in the Holy Book the Bhagavad-Geetā, one of the Upanishads, in the Science of the Supreme Spirit, in the Art of Self-Knowledge, in the colloquy between the Divine Lord Shri Krishna and the Prince Arjuna, stands the sixteenth chapter, entitled: Divine and Demoniac Civilisation.

CHAPTER XVII

★

Arjuna asked: 'My Lord! Those who do acts of sacrifice, not according to the scriptures but nevertheless with implicit faith, what is their condition? Is it one of Purity, of Passion or of Ignorance?'

Lord Shri Krishna replied: 'Man has an inherent faith in one or other of the Qualities—Purity, Passion and Ignorance. Now listen.

'The faith of every man conforms to his nature. By nature he is full of faith. He is in fact what his faith makes him.

'The Pure worship the true God; the Passionate, the powers of wealth and magic; the Ignorant, the spirits of the dead and of the lower orders of nature.

'Those who practise austerities not commanded by scripture, who are slaves to hypocrisy and egotism, who are carried away by the fury of desire and passion,

'They are ignorant. They torment the organs of the body; and they harass Me also, Who lives within. Know that they are devoted to evil.

'The food which men enjoy is also threefold, like the ways of sacrifice, austerity and almsgiving. Listen to the distinction.

'The foods that prolong life and increase purity, vigour, health, cheerfulness and happiness are those that are delicious, soothing, substantial and agreeable. These are loved by the Pure.

'Those in whom Passion is dominant like foods that are

bitter, sour, salt, over-hot, pungent, dry and burning. These produce unhappiness, repentance and disease.

'The Ignorant love food which is stale, not nourishing, putrid and corrupt, the leavings of others and unclean.

'Sacrifice is Pure, when it is offered by one who does not covet the fruit thereof, when it is done according to the commands of scripture, and with implicit faith that the sacrifice is a duty.

'Sacrifice which is performed for the sake of its results, or for self-glorification—that, O best of Āryans! is the product of Passion.

'Sacrifice that is contrary to scriptural command, that is unaccompanied by prayers or gifts of food or money, and is without faith—that is the product of Ignorance.

'Worship of God and the Master; respect for the preacher and the philosopher; purity, rectitude, continence and harmlessness—all this is physical austerity.

'Speech that hurts no one, that is true, is pleasant to listen to and beneficial, and the constant study of the scriptures— this is austerity in speech.

'Serenity, kindness, silence, self-control and purity—this is austerity of mind.

'These threefold austerities performed with faith, and without thought of reward, may truly be accounted Pure.

'Austerity coupled with hypocrisy or performed for the sake of self-glorification, popularity or vanity, comes from Passion, and its result is always doubtful and temporary.

'Austerity done under delusion, and accompanied with sorcery or torture to oneself or another, may be assumed to spring from Ignorance.

'The gift which is given without thought of recompense, in the belief that it ought to be made, in a fit place, at an opportune time and to a deserving person—such a gift is Pure.

'That which is given for the sake of the results it will produce, or with the hope of recompense, or grudgingly—that may truly be said to be the outcome of Passion.

'And that which is given at an unsuitable place or time or to one who is unworthy, or with disrespect or contempt—such a gift is the result of Ignorance.

' "Ôm Tat Sat"—is the triple designation of the Eternal Spirit, by which of old the Vedic scriptures, the ceremonials and the sacrifices were ordained.

Therefore all acts of sacrifice, gifts and austerities, prescribed by the scriptures, are always begun by those who understand the Spirit with the word Ôm.

'Those who desire deliverance begin their acts of sacrifice, austerity or gift with the word "Tat" (meaning "That"), without thought of reward.

' "Sat" means Reality or the highest Good, and also, O Arjuna! it is used to mean an action of exceptional merit.

'Conviction in sacrifice, in austerity and in giving is also called "Sat". So too an action done only for the Lord's sake.

'Whatsoever is done without faith, whether it be sacrifice, austerity or gift or anything else, is called "Asat" (meaning "Unreal")—for it is the negation of "Sat", O Arjuna! Such an act has no significance, here or hereafter

Thus, in the Holy Book the Bhagavad-Geetā, one of the Upanishads, in the Science of the Supreme Spirit, in the Art of Self-Knowledge, in the colloquy between the Divine Lord Shri Krishna and the Prince Arjuna, stands the seventeenth chapter, entitled: The Threefold Faith.

CHAPTER XVIII

★

Arjuna asked: 'O Mighty One! I desire to know how relinquishing is distinguished from renunciation.'

Lord Shri Krishna replied: 'The sages say that renunciation means forgoing an action which springs from desire; and relinquishing means the surrender of its fruit.

'Some philosophers say that all action is evil, and should be abandoned. Others that acts of sacrifice, benevolence and austerity should not be given up.

'O best of Indians! Listen to my judgment as regards this problem. It has a threefold aspect.

'Acts of sacrifice, benevolence and austerity should not be given up, but should be performed; for they purify the aspiring soul.

'But they should be done with detachment, and without thought of recompense. This is my final judgment.

'It is not right to give up actions which are obligatory; and if they are misunderstood and ignored, it is the result of sheer ignorance.

'To avoid an action through fear of physical suffering, because it is likely to be painful, is to act from passion, and the benefit of renunciation will not follow.

'He who performs an obligatory action, because he believes it to be a duty which ought to be done, without any personal desire either to do the act or to receive any return—such renunciation is Pure.

'The wise man who has attained purity, whose doubts are solved, who is filled with the spirit of self-abnegation, does not shrink from action because it brings pain, nor does he desire it because it brings pleasure.

'But since those still in the body cannot entirely avoid action, in their case abandonment of the fruit of action is considered as complete renunciation.

'For those who cannot renounce all desire, the fruit of action hereafter is threefold—good, evil, and partly good and partly evil. But for him who has renounced, there is none.

'I will tell thee now, O Mighty Man! the five causes which, according to the final decision of philosophy, must concur before an action can be accomplished.

'They are a body, a personality, physical organs, their manifold activity, and destiny.

'Whatever action a man perform, whether by muscular effort or by speech or by thought, and whether it be right or wrong, these five are the essential causes.

'But the fool who supposes, because of his immature judgment, that it is his own Self alone that acts, he perverts the truth, and does not see rightly.

'He who has no pride, and whose intellect is unalloyed by attachment, even though he kill these people, yet he does not kill them, and his act does not bind him.

'Knowledge, the knower, and the object of knowledge, these are the threefold incentives to action; and the act, the actor and the instrument are the threefold constituents.

'The knowledge, the act and the doer differ according to the Qualities. Listen to this too:

'That knowledge which sees the One Indestructible in all beings, the One Indivisible in all separate lives, may be truly called Pure Knowledge.

'The knowledge which thinks of the manifold existence in all beings as separate—that comes from Passion.

'But that which clings blindly to one idea as if it were all, without logic, truth or insight, that has its origin in Darkness.

'An obligatory action done by one who is disinterested, who neither likes it nor dislikes it, and gives no thought to the consequences that follow, such an action is Pure.

'But even though an action involve the most strenuous endeavour, yet if the doer is seeking to gratify his desires, and is filled with personal vanity, it may be assumed to originate in Passion.

'An action undertaken through delusion, and with no regard to the spiritual issues involved, or to the real capacity of the doer, or to the injury which may follow, such an act may be assumed to be the product of Ignorance.

'But when a man has no sentiment and no personal vanity, when he possesses courage and confidence, cares not whether he succeeds or fails, then his action arises from Purity.

'In him who is impulsive, greedy, looking for reward, violent, impure, torn between joy and sorrow, it may be assumed that in him Passion is predominant.

'While he whose purpose is infirm, who is low-minded, stubborn, dishonest, malicious, indolent, despondent, procrastinating—he may be assumed to be in Darkness.

'Reason and conviction are threefold, according to the Quality which is dominant. I will explain them fully and severally, O Arjuna!

'That intellect which understands the creation and dissolution of life, what actions should be done and what not, which discriminates between fear and fearlessness, bondage and deliverance, that is Pure.

90

'The intellect which does not understand what is right and what is wrong, and what should be done and what not, is under the sway of Passion.

'And that which, shrouded in Ignorance, thinks wrong right, and sees everything perversely, O Arjuna! that intellect is ruled by Darkness.

'The conviction and steady concentration by which the mind, the vitality and the senses are controlled —O Arjuna! they are the product of Purity.

'The conviction which always holds fast to rituals, to self-interest and wealth, for the sake of what they may bring forth—that comes from Passion.

'And that which clings perversely to false idealism, fear, grief, despair and vanity—it is the product of Ignorance.

'Hear further the three kinds of pleasure. That which increases day after day and delivers one from misery,

'Which at first seems like poison but afterwards acts like nectar—that pleasure is Pure, for it is born of Wisdom.

'That which at first is like nectar, because the senses revel in their objects, but in the end acts like poison—that pleasure arises from Passion.

'While the pleasure which from first to last merely drugs the senses, which springs from indolence, lethargy and folly—that pleasure flows from Ignorance.

'There is nothing anywhere on earth or in the higher worlds which is free from the three Qualities—for they are born of Nature.

'O Arjuna! The duties of the spiritual teachers, the soldiers, the traders and the servants, have all been fixed according to the dominant Quality in their nature.

'Serenity, self-restraint, austerity, purity, forgiveness, as well as uprightness, knowledge, wisdom, and faith in God— these constitute the duty of a spiritual Teacher.

'Valour, glory, firmness, skill, generosity, steadiness in battle, and ability to rule—these constitute the duty of a soldier. They flow from his own nature.

'Agriculture, protection of the cow and trade, are the duty of a trader; again in accordance with his nature. The duty of a servant is to serve, and that too agrees with his nature.

'Perfection is attained when each attends diligently to his duty. Listen and I will tell you how it is attained by him who always minds his own duty.

'Man reaches perfection by dedicating his actions to God, Who is the source of all being, and fills everything.

'It is better to do one's own duty, however defective it may be, than to follow the duty of another, however well one may perform it. He who does his duty as his own nature reveals it, never sins.

'The duty that of itself falls to one's lot should not be abandoned, though it may have its defects. All acts are marred by defects, as fire is obscured by smoke.

'He whose mind is entirely detached, who has conquered himself, whose desires have vanished, by his renunciation reaches that stage of perfect freedom where action completes itself and leaves no seed.

'I will now state briefly how he, who has reached perfection, finds the Eternal Spirit, the state of Supreme Wisdom.

'Guided always by pure reason, bravely restraining himself, renouncing the objects of sense, and giving up attachment and hatred;

'Enjoying solitude, abstemious, his body, mind and speech under perfect control, absorbed in meditation, he becomes free—always filled with the spirit of renunciation.

'Having abandoned selfishness, power, arrogance, anger and desire, possessing nothing of his own, and having attained peace, he is fit to join the Eternal Spirit.

'And when he becomes one with the Eternal, and his soul knows the bliss that belongs to the Self, he feels no desire and no regret, he regards all beings equally, and enjoys the blessing of supreme devotion to Me.

'By such devotion, he sees Me, who I am and what I am; and thus realising the Truth, he enters My Kingdom.

'Relying on Me in all his actions and doing them for My sake, he attains, by My Grace, Eternal and Unchangeable Life.

'Surrender then thy actions unto Me, live in Me, concentrate thine intellect on Me, and think always of Me.

'Fix but thy mind on Me, and by My grace thou shalt overcome the obstacles in thy path. But if, misled by pride, thou wilt not listen, then indeed thou shalt be lost.

'If thou in thy vanity thinkest of avoiding this fight, thy will shall not be fulfilled, for Nature herself will compel thee.

'O Arjuna! Thy duty binds Thee. From thine own nature has it arisen, and that which in thy delusion thou desirest not to do, that very thing thou shalt do. Thou art helpless.

'God dwells in the hearts of all beings, O Arjuna! He causes them to revolve as it were on a wheel by His mystic power.

'With all thy strength, fly unto Him, and surrender thyself, and by His grace shalt thou attain Supreme Peace, and reach the Eternal Home.

'Thus have I revealed to thee the Truth, the Mystery of mysteries. Having thought over it, thou art free to act as thou wilt.

'Only listen once more to My last word, the deepest secret of all; thou art My beloved, thou art My friend, and I speak for thy welfare.

'Dedicate thyself to Me, worship Me, sacrifice all for Me,

prostrate thyself before Me, and to Me thou shalt surely come. Truly do I pledge thee; thou art My own beloved.

'Give up then thy earthly duties, surrender thyself to Me only. Do not be anxious; I will absolve thee from all thy sin.

'Speak not this to one who has not practised austerities, or to him who does not love, or who will not listen, or who mocks.

'But he who teaches this great secret to My devotees, his is the highest devotion, and verily he shall come unto Me.

'Nor is there among men any who can perform a service dearer to Me than this, or any man on earth more beloved by Me than he.

'He who will study this spiritual discourse of ours, I assure thee, he shall thereby worship Me at the altar of Wisdom.

'Yea, he who listens to it with faith, and without doubt, even he, freed from evil, shall rise to the worlds which the virtuous attain through righteous deeds.

'O Arjuna! Hast thou listened attentively to My words? Has thy ignorance and thy delusion gone?'

Arjuna replied: 'My Lord! O Immutable One! My delusion has fled. By Thy Grace, O Changeless One, the light has dawned. My doubts are gone, and I stand before Thee ready to do Thy will.'

Sanjaya told: Thus have I heard this rare, wonderful and soul-stirring discourse of the Lord Shri Krishna and the great-souled Arjuna.

Through the blessing of the sage Vyāsa, I listened to this secret and noble science from the lips of its Master, the Lord Shri Krishna.

O King! The more I think of that marvellous and holy discourse, the more I lose myself in joy.

As memory recalls again and again the exceeding beauty of the Lord, I am filled with amazement and happiness.

Wherever is the Lord Shri Krishna, the Prince of Wisdom, and wherever is Arjuna, the Great Archer, I am more than convinced that good fortune, victory, happiness and right-eousness will follow.

Thus, in the Holy Book the Bhagavad-Geetā, one of the Upanishads, in the Science of the Supreme Spirit, in the Art of Self-Knowledge, in the colloquy between the Divine Lord Shri Krishna and the Prince Arjuna, stands the eighteenth chapter, entitled: Spirit of Renunciation.

May the Lord Shri Krishna bless you!